Each Day a New Beginning

Compiled by Michael Ryan
Cover Design By Bridgewater Design Consultants
Cover Art By B.Hammerman Brody

ISBN 1-56245-046-8

Printed in Hong Kong

Great Quotations Publishing Company
1967 Quincy Court
Glendale Heights, Illinois 60139

Look to this day, for it is life,
the very life of life: In it's brief
course lie all the realities and verities
of existence; the bliss of growth, the splendor
of action, the glory of power...

For yesterday is but a dream, and tomorrow is only
a vision, but today, well lived, makes every
yesterday a dream of happiness and every
tomorrow a vision of hope.

Sanskrit Proverb

EACH DAY
a new beginning

Phone Numbers

Phone Numbers

_____

_____

_____

_____

_____

_____

_____

_____

_____

_____

_____

_____

_____

_____

Phone Numbers

Phone Numbers

_____

_____

_____

_____

_____

_____

_____

_____

_____

_____

_____

_____

_____

Phone Numbers

_____

_____

_____

_____

_____

_____

_____

_____

_____

_____

_____

_____

_____

Birthdays

Birthdays

Birthdays

Birthdays

_____

_____

_____

_____

_____

_____

_____

_____

_____

_____

_____

_____

_____

_____

Special Occasions

Special Occasions

_____

_____

_____

_____

_____

_____

_____

_____

_____

_____

_____

_____

_____

_____

I take it to be a principle of life,
not to be too much addicted
to any one thing.

Terence

January 1

There is always one moment in childhood
when the door opens and
lets the future in.

Graham Greene

December 31

Thought for the Day

I am grateful for life's
generosity to me.
I am blessed.

January 2

Change is always powerful.
Let your hook be always cast.
In the pool where you least
expect it, will be a fish.

Ovid (43 B.C. - C.A.D. 17)

December 30

The universe is transformation;
our life is what our thoughts make it.

Marcus Aurelius Antonius

January 3

The best way to make your dreams
come true is to wake up.

Paul Valery

December 29

Remember, one thought
does not mean much.
But thoughts that we think over and over
are like drops of water:
at first there are just a few;
and then after awhile you've
created a pool...then a lake...
and then an ocean.

January 4

People change and forget to tell each other.

Lillian Hellman

December 28

It may be those who do most,
dream most.

Stephen Leacock

January 5

Thought for the Day

Today I will welcome my dreams.
They indicate tomorrows successful ventures.

December 27

The distance doesn't matter;
only the first step is difficult.

Mme. du Deffand

January 6

A true friend is the most precious of
all possessions and the one we take the
least thought about acquiring.

La Rochefoucauld (1613-1680)

December 26

Nothing is permanent -
except change.

January 7

I am more afraid of my own heart
than of the Pope and all his cardinals.
I have within me the great Pope, Self.

Martin Luther

December 25

One cannot collect all the
beautiful shells on the beach,
one can collect only a few.

Anne Morrow Lindbergh

January 8

We can scare ourselves or inspire ourselves... We are the architects of our own attitudes and experiences. We design the world by the way we choose to see it.

Barry Neil Kaufman

December 24

Hope is a good breakfast, but it is a bad supper.

Francis Bacon

January 9

I can't think of any sorrow in the world
that a hot bath wouldn't help,
just a little bit.

Susan Glaspell

December 23

There's a period of life when we
swallow a knowledge of ourselves
and it becomes either good
or sour inside.

Pearl Bailey

January 10

People have to learn sometimes not only
how much the heart, but how much
the head, can bear.

Maria Mitchell

December 22

Opportunities to be generous of spirit
are always present.

January 11

It is while trying to get everything
straight in my head that I get confused.

Mary Virginia Micka

December 21

Genuine beginnings begin with us,
even when they are brought to our
attention by external opportunities.

William Bridges

January 12

Thought for the Day

I will try to be calmer today and see if it has a positive effect on those around me.

December 20

... a joy will open our hearts
like a flower, enabling us to
enter the world of reality.

Thich Nhat Hanh

January 13

All life is the struggle, the effort to be itself. The difficulties which I meet with in order to realize my existence are precisely what awaken and mobilize my activities, my capacities.

Jose Ortega y Gasset

December 19

Our hearts often know quickly
what our minds find out eventually.

January 14

The Saints are Sinners who keep on trying.

Robert Louis Stevenson

December 18

Most people fail because they
do not wake and see when they
stand at the fork in the road
and have to decide.

Erich Fromm

January 15

It is sad not to be loved,
but it is much sadder not
to be able to love.

Miguel de Unamuno

December 17

If we try too hard to force
others to live in our world,
because we think it is the real world,
we are doomed to disappointment.

William Glasser, M.D.

January 16

Thought for the Day

What life offers today is what I need -
no matter what I may think.

December 16

...fear makes strangers of people
who should be friends.

Shirley McLaine

January 17

I am imagination. I can see what the eyes cannot see. I can hear what the ears cannot hear. I can feel what the heart cannot feel.

Peter Nivio Zarlenga

December 15

Experience is a good teacher, but she sends in terrific bills.

Minna Antrim

January 18

At every step the child should be allowed
to meet the real experiences of life;
the thorns should never be
plucked from the roses.

Ellen Key

December 14

There is nothing so moving -
not even acts of love or hate -
as the discovery that one is not alone.

Robert Ardrey

January 19

Imagine there's no country.
It isn't hard to do.
Nothing to kill or die for.
And no religion, too.

John Lennon

December 13

The starting point for fun is
believing you deserve to have it.

January 20

God, give us the grace to accept with serenity the things that cannot be changed, courage to change the things which could be changed, and the wisdom to distinguish the one from the other.

Reinhold Niebuhr

December 12

We are whole beings.
We know this somewhere in a part
of ourselves that feels like memory.

Susan Griffin

January 21

Wherever I am, in the twisting road of my life,
is where I'm meant to be.

December 11

Only a life lived for others
is the life worthwhile.

Albert Einstein

January 22

Thought for the Day

I'll be conscious today of my self-talk.
My experiences will directly
reflect my thoughts.

December 10

Thought for the Day

Peace with self is a
treasure beyond measure.

January 23

Everything that irritates us about others
can lead us to an understanding of ourselves.

Carl Jung

December 9

Don't hurry, don't worry.
You're only here for a short visit.
So be sure to stop and
smell the flowers.

Walter Hagen

January 24

We live in a fantasy world,
a world of illusion.
The great task in life is to find reality.

Iris Murdoch

December 8

Don't worry about
avoiding temptation.
As you grow older, it will avoid you.

Joey Adams

January 25

Today I will try not to get so caught up
in activities that I miss the
beauty around me.

December 7

Life is made up of sobs, sniffles, and smiles, with sniffles predominating.

O. Henry

January 26

We are all born for love.
It is the principle of existence,
and its only end.

Benjamin Disraeli

December 6

I must accept and work around
my limitations if I am
to have a happy life.

January 27

Love and skill together can
create a miracle.

December 5

All our dreams can come true if we have the courage to pursue them.

Walt Disney

January 28

Today, I'll look within and seek
to please myself.

December 4

It is better to ask some questions
than to know all the answers.

James Thurber

January 29

Knowledge is the process of piling up facts.
Wisdom lies in their simplification.

Martin H. Fischer

December 3

Thought for the Day

Ultimately I am what I choose to be;
my self-esteem follows the same path.

January 30

The day promises challenge and
many choices. I can successfully
handle all possibilities.

December 2

Success requires that I push my
surface emotions out of the drivers seat.

January 31

If one is going to change things,
one has to make a fuss and catch
the eye of the world.

Elizabeth Janeway

December 1

Try to keep the rebel artist alive in you,
no matter how attractive or
exhausting the temptation.

Norman Mailer

February 1

I have a right to my anger,
and I don't want anybody
telling me I shouldn't be,
that it's not nice to be,
and that something's wrong with me
because I get angry.

Maxine Waters

November 30

I will take today slowly and easily.
If a struggle develops, I will cherish it.
It means growth.

February 2

In going through the checkout lane of life,
the person to watch is the person
behind the person in front of you.

Anonymous

November 29

When you have become willing
to hide nothing, you will not only
be willing to enter into communion
but will also understand peace and joy.

Anonymous

February 3

Relationships are only as alive as
the people engaging in them.

Donald B Ardell

November 28

I don't want to live -
I want to love first,
and live incidentally.

Zelda Fitzgerald

February 4

Thought for the Day

Today I will welcome my dreams.
They indicate tomorrows' successful ventures.

November 27

The whole secret of a successful life
is to find out what is one's destiny to do,
and then do it.

Henry Ford

February 5

Thought for the Day

I will set aside my judgment of others
and concentrate instead on freeing myself.

November 26

It is not what we see and touch
or that which others do for us which
makes us happy; it is that which
we think and feel and do,
first for the other fellow
and then for ourselves.

Helen Keller

February 6

God creates.
People rearrange.

Joseph Casey

November 25

Thought for the Day

I can answer yes to today and
all it offers, and be at peace.

February 7

Can I stay with the moment and the activity before me, just for today?

November 24

Any path is only a path,
and there is no affront,
to oneself or to others,
in dropping if that is what
your heart tells you.

Carlos Castaneda

February 8

Our grand business in life is not
to see what lies dimly at a distance,
but to do what lies clearly at hand.

Thomas Caryle

November 23

Within our dreams and aspirations we find opportunities.

Sue Atchley Ebaugh

February 9

Be great in act, as you have been in thought.
Suit the action to the word,
and the word to the action.

William Shakespeare

November 22

The most prophetic utterances have emanated from the most poetical minds.

William F. R. Stanley

February 10

It is of immense importance to learn
to laugh at ourselves.

Katherine Mansfield

November 21

I may need to redefine happiness,
rather than put it on hold.

February 11

Today I look beyond the challenges in
my life and use my energy productively.

November 20

There are two tragedies in life.
One is not to get your heart's desire.
The other is to get it.

George Bernard Shaw

February 12

Love is an act of faith, and whoever is
of little faith is also of little love.

Erich Fromm

November 19

I like to listen. I have learned a great deal from listening carefully. Most people never listen.

Ernest Hemingway

February 13

Even a thought, even a possibility
can shatter us and transform us.

Nietzsche

November 18

Thought for the Day

All is well. I'm ready for
whatever comes today.
My yesterdays have prepared me.

February 14

Never bend your head, always hold it high.
Look the world straight in the face.

Helen Keller

November 17

A belief which does not spring
from a conviction in the
emotions is no belief at all.

Evelyn Scott

February 15

If I am honest with myself,
I can be my own best teacher.

November 16

Of course, fortune has its
part in human affairs,
but conduct is really
much more important.

Jeanne Detourbey

February 16

Live each day as if your life had just begun.

Goethe

November 15

Dreams are...illustrations from the book your soul is writing about you.

Marsha Norman

February 17

I know God will not give me
anything I can't handle.
I just wish He didn't trust me so much.

Mother Teresa

November 14

In the transformation and
growth of all things,
every bud and feature
has its proper form.

Fritjof Capra

February 18

Do not forget little kindnesses and
do not remember small faults.

Chinese Proverb

November 13

Our deeds still travel with us from afar,
And what we have been
makes us what we are.

George Eliot

February 19

Always hold fast to the present.
Every situation, indeed every moment,
is of infinite value, for it is the
representation of a whole eternity.

Johann Wolfgang von Goethe

November 12

I embrace my experience now
as part of my learning process.

February 20

Thought for the Day

The first step towards unconditional love
is accepting others as they are.

November 11

... the absence of love in our lives
is what makes them seem
raw and unfinished.

Ingrid Bengis

February 21

Thought for the Day

Stay young by remaining flexible,
adaptable and open-minded.
Don't let your "mental" arteries harden.

November 10

It is good to have an end
to journey towards;
but it is the journey that matters,
in the end.

Ursala K. LeGuin

February 22

I can sometimes resist temptation,
but never mischief.

Joyce Rebeta-Burditt

November 9

I will try to be able to say
of my work today,
"I would do this even if
I weren't paid for it."

February 23

God is a comedian whose audience is afraid to laugh.

H.L. Mencken

November 8

I've arrived at this outermost edge
of my life by my own actions.
Where I am is thoroughly unacceptable.
Therefore, I must stop doing
what I've been doing.

Alice Koller

February 24

Beauty is in the eye of the beholder.

November 7

If you would be loved,
love and be lovable.

Benjamin Franklin

February 25

Naked we were born and
naked we must depart...
No matter what you lose,
be patient for nothing belongs;
it is only lent.

Gluckel of Hameln

November 6

All great reforms require one to dare a lot to win a little.

William L. O'Neill

February 26

Mystic: A person who is puzzled
before the obvious, but who
understands the nonexistent.

November 5

There is a sanctuary
in my own heart.

February 27

Taking a few stress breaks every day
helps me keep my perspective.

It is time to show the strength
of water and flow away....
To stand is to be crushed,
but to flow out is to gather new strength.

Marge Piercy

February 28

Today I will try to experience my life
through the eyes of a child.

November 3

If you can imagine it, you can achieve it.
If you can dream it, you can become it.

William Arthur Ward

February 29

Thought for the Day

With the power of your
creative imagination,
you can catch a vision...
you can dream the dream!

November 2

Paradoxical as it may seem,
to believe in youth is to look backward;
to look forward we must believe in age.

Dorothy L. Sayers

March 1

If a man speaks or acts with pure thought,
happiness follows him like a shadow
that never leaves him.

Buddha

November 1

The miracle comes quietly into the mind
than stops an instant and is still.
A Course in Miracles.

March 2

Different perceptions
create different options.

October 31

Hold fast to dreams for if dreams die, life is a broken winged bird that cannot fly.

Langston Hughes

March 3

Thought for the Day

Today I am learning to think and act
in a positive way that is healthy
for my mind, body and spirit.

October 30

Thought for the Day

Let's be sure that what I desire
is worthy of my best self.

March 4

I must trust my inner voice.
I am strong, wise, and powerful.

October 29

One has to have a bit of neurosis
to go on being an artist.
A balanced human seldom produces art.
It's that imbalance which impels us.

Beverly Pepper

March 5

The greater part of our happiness or misery
depends on our dispositions and not
on our circumstances.

Martha Washington

October 28

The brain is a wonderful organ;
it starts working the moment you
get up in the morning and does not stop
until you get to the office.

Robert Frost

March 6

Thought for the Day

I am very grateful for the gift of this day.
It is mine to do exactly what I choose
and I choose to use it for good and love.

October 27

I am free today to be who I want to be.
To grow or not to grow. To feel joy or pain.

March 7

We judge ourselves by what we feel capable of doing, while others judge us by what we have already done.

Henry Wadsworth Longfellow

October 26

To share often and much...
to know even one life has breathed
easier because you have lived.
This is to have succeeded.

Ralph Waldo Emerson

March 8

There is no cure for birth or death,
save to enjoy the interval.

George Santayana

October 25

The beauty of the world...has two edges,
one of laughter, one of anguish,
cutting the heart asunder.

Virginia Woolf

March 9

Illusions are art for the feeling person,
and it is by art that we live, if we do.

Elizabeth Bowen

October 24

Over the years our bodies become
walking autobiographies,
telling friends and strangers alike
of the minor and major stresses of our lives.

Marilyn Ferguson

March 10

Nature never repeats herself,
and the possibilities of one human soul
will never be found in another.

Elizabeth Cady Stanton

October 23

Thought for the Day

I will love someone fully today
and I'll understand their meaning in my life.

March 11

My life is increasingly an inner one and
the outer setting matters less and less.

Etty Hillesum

October 22

Life comes in clusters, clusters of solitude,
then a cluster when there is
hardly time to breathe.

May Sarton

March 12

If we go down into ourselves we find
that we possess exactly what we desire.

Simone Weil

October 21

Inside myself is a place where I
live all alone and that's where you
renew your springs that never dry up.

Pearl S. Buck

March 13

Today I choose to stay in the reality
of my life and feel all there is to feel.

October 20

I am the expert on my own life.
Today and every day let me
be wise enough to consult myself.

March 14

There are two ways of spreading light:
to be the candle or the mirror that reflects it.

Edith Wharton

October 19

Thought for the Day

Today I will decide to be fully
human in all my encounters.

March 15

To jealously, nothing is more frightful than laughter.

Francoise Sagan

October 18

In every man's heart, there is a
secret nerve that answers to
the vibrations of beauty.

Christopher Morley

March 16

I postpone death by living, by suffering,
by error, by risking, by giving, by losing.

Anais Nin

October 17

We will be victorious if we have not forgotten to learn.

Rosa Luxemburg

March 17

Be gentle with yourself, learn to love yourself,
to forgive yourself, for only as we have
the right attitude toward ourselves
can we have the right attitude toward others.

October 16

Trouble is a sieve through which we
sift our acquaintances.
Those too big to pass through
are our friends.

Arlene Francis

March 18

I was merely a disinterested spectator
at the Banquet of Life.

Elaine Dundy

October 15

Thought for the Day

My love is best expressed when I help someone else live life more comfortably.

March 19

Every day look at a beautiful picture,
read a beautiful poem, listen to
some beautiful music, and if possible,
say some reasonable thing.

Goethe

October 14

The way to love anything is to
realize it might be lost.

G. K. Chesterton

March 20

There's only one corner of the universe
you can be certain of improving
and that's your own self.

Aldous Huxley

October 13

However much we guard against it,
we tend to shape ourselves in
the image others have of us.

Eric Hoffer

March 21

I have never found the companion
that was so companionable as solitude.

Henry David Thoreau

October 12

All I have seen teaches me to
trust the creator for all I have not seen.

Ralph Waldo Emerson

March 22

The easiest kind of relationship
for me is with 10,000 people.
The hardest is with one.

Joan Baez

October 11

Thought for the Day

No event need throw me today.
And yet, every situation offers me
a chance to practice healthy living.

March 23

I easily flow with change.
My life is guided and I am always
going in the right direction.

October 10

The person that knows how to laugh
at himself will never cease to be amused.

Shirley MacLaine

March 24

What you dislike in another take care to correct in yourself.

Thomas Sprat

October 9

Better keep yourself clean and bright;
you are the window through which
you must see the world.

George Bernard Shaw

March 25

A human being isn't an orchid,
he must draw something from
the soil he grows in.

Sara Jeannette Duncan

October 8

Treasure the love you receive above all.
It will survive long after your gold
and good health have vanished.

Og Mandino

March 26

Thought for the Day

I am letting go of pushing myself.
I can achieve my goals in life in a relaxed way.

October 7

To find out what I hold most precious,
I will try to imagine giving it up.

March 27

Home is not where you live but where they understand you.

Christian Morgenstern

October 6

....all humans are frightened of
their own solitude. Yet only in
solitude can we learn to know ourselves,
learn to handle our own
eternity of aloneness.

Han Suyin

March 28

Happiness is essentially a state
of going somewhere, wholeheartedly,
one-directional, without regret or reservation.

William H. Sheldon

October 5

To expect life to be tailored to
our specifications is to invite frustration.

Unknown

March 29

Most of all, learn to laugh at yourself;
meet each day with a sense of humor.

October 4

I can act at every moment in such a way
as to honor the past and
enhance the future.

March 30

Without friends no one would choose to live, though he had all other goods.

Aristotle

October 3

The solution to my life occurred to me one evening while I was ironing a shirt.

Alice Munro

March 31

It is in his pleasure that a man really lives;
it is from his leisure that he constructs
the true fabric of self.

Agnes Repplier

October 2

Happiness is a by-product of an effort to make somebody else happy.

Gretta Brooker Palmer

April 1

I am never afraid of what I know.

Anna Sewell

October 1

I don't wait for moods.
You accomplish nothing if you do that.
Your mind must know it has
got to get down to earth.

Pearl S. Buck

April 2

I am one of those who never knows the
direction of my journey until
I have almost arrived.

Anna Louise Strong

September 30

Take time to notice how amazing
your world truly is.

April 3

Thought for the Day

Today I'll strive to clear my path and to appreciate the perfection of each moment that I choose.

September 29

The inner voice can be heard
if I choose to listen.
It will never guide me wrongly.

April 4

Character builds slowly,
but it can be torn down
with incredible swiftness.

Faith Baldwin

September 28

One often learns more from ten days
of agony than from ten years
of contentment.

Merle Shain

April 5

The tragedy of life is that people do not change.

Agatha Christie

September 27

I am ashamed of these tears.
And yet at the extreme of my misfortune
I am ashamed not to shed them.

Euripides

April 6

Thought for the Day

I will endeavor to accept my life;
it is taking me where I need to go.

September 26

Today I celebrate my
greater openness with others.

April 7

My great mistake, the fault for which I
can't forgive myself, is that one day
I ceased my obstinate pursuit
of my own individuality.

Oscar Wilde

September 25

If there's something to do, then do it.
If not, relax and have fun.

April 8

There are limits to self-indulgence, none to self-restraint.

Gandhi

September 24

Noble deeds and hot baths are the best cures for depression.

Dodie Smith

April 9

Today I will risk showing
myself as I really am.

September 23

The heart is happiest
when it beats for others.

April 10

Compassion for myself is the most powerful healer of them all.

Theodore Isaac Rubin

September 22

Thought for the Day

I will not let fear keep me from
the treasures of the heart.

April 11

Be yourself. Who else is better qualified?

Frank J. Giblin, II

September 21

Some things...arrive on their own
mysterious hour, on their own terms
and not yours, to be seized
or relinquished forever.

Gail Godwin

April 12

Thought for the Day

Today, I will try new places ,
read new books,
try new hobbies.

September 20

We don't see things as they are,
we see them as we are.

Anais Nin

April 13

We judge ourselves by our motives
and others by their actions.

Dwight Morrow

September 19

No one but me determines
my course today.
My success begins in my mind.

April 14

I have never seen a greater monster
or miracle in the world than myself.

Montaigne

September 18

Every step you take should move you
in the direction of your vision.

April 15

Thought for the Day

I will celebrate my personal power
and use it to my advantage. Today!

September 17

Relationships are only as alive as the
people engaging in them.

Donald B. Ardell

April 16

Everything in life that we really accept
undergoes a change.

Katherine Mansfield

September 16

To live in dialogue with another
is to live twice.
Joys are doubled by exchange
and burdens are cut in half.

Wishart

April 17

I love my past. I love my present.
I'm not ashamed of what I've had,
and I'm not sad because I have it no longer.

Colette

September 15

I think I must let go. Must fear not, must be quiet so that my children can hear the Sound of Creation and dance the dance that is in them.

Russel Hoban

April 18

Thought for the Day

When I listen to my own truth
I will be guided truly.

September 14

To keep your character intact
you cannot stoop to filthy acts.
It makes it easier to stoop the next time.

Katherine Hepburn

April 19

It is the function of vice to keep virtue within reasonable grounds.

Samuel Butler

September 13

I have absolute freedom to
choose in every instant.

April 20

Truth is something you stumble into
when you think you're going some place else.

Jerry Garcia

September 12

I dream my painting,
and then I paint my dreams.

Vincent Van Gogh

April 21

Today, I will select the colors of my thoughts; drab or bright, weak or strong, good or bad.

Accept your partner's limits,
and stay or go based on your own.

April 22

The truth is cruel, but it can be loved,
and it makes free those who have loved it.

George Santayana

September 10

Thought for the Day

Only by letting go of life do I most profoundly enhance it.

April 23

It is characteristic of wisdom not
to do desperate things.

Henry David Thoreau

September 9

Happiness sneaks in through a door you didn't know you left open.

John Barrymore

April 24

Make voyages. Attempt them.
There's nothing else.

Tennessee Williams

September 8

I have learned silence from the talkative; tolerance from the intolerant and kindness from the unkind. I should not be ungrateful to those teachers.

Kahlil Gibran

April 25

Thought for the Day

Today, I will set up personal incentives -
promising myself rewards for work completed.

September 7

Today, I will try to reach out to people
who share my interest.

April 26

I have met with women who I really think
would like to be married to a poem,
and to be given away by a novel.

John Keats

September 6

Today, I will make an effort to be fully conscious
of the motives behind my actions.

April 27

The limits of my language mean the limits of my world.

Ludwig Wittgenstein

September 5

The best and most beautiful things
in the world cannot be seen,
nor touched.... but are felt in the heart.

Helen Keller

April 28

Not all gifts are love and joy.
Let me respect the gifts of grief and silence,
that I may learn from them.

September 4

If you shut your door to all errors,
truth will be shut out.

Rabindranath Tagore

April 29

The strongest principle of growth lies in the human choice.

George Eliot

September 3

Slow down. There's nothing
more precious than now.

April 30

Green is the fresh emblem of
well-founded hopes. In blue,
the spirit can wander, but in green it can rest.

Mary Webb

September 2

Thought for the Day

Today I will try to spend more time
thinking about life's pleasures.
I've neglected them for too long.

May 1

Thought for the Day

Today, I'll listen to the notes of others,
and find my harmony with them.

September 1

The game of life is a game of boomerangs.
Our thoughts, deeds, and words return
to us sooner or later,
with astounding accuracy.

Florence Scovel Shinn

May 2

When we are writing, or painting,
or composing, we are, during the
time of creativity, freed from
normal restrictions, and are
opened to a wider world, where colors
are brighter, sounds clearer, and people more won-
drously complex than we normally realize.

Madeleine L'Engle

August 31

I search in these words and find nothing
more than myself, caught between
the grapes and the thorns.

Anne Sexton

May 3

Dreams say what they mean,
but they don't say it in a daytime language.

Gail Godwin

August 30

Speak your truth quietly and clearly;
and listen to others,
even to the dull and the ignorant;
they too have their story.

Max Ehrmann

May 4

Thought for the Day

Today, I will keep my heart young
and my expectations high
and keep my dreams alive.

August 29

You must not change one thing,
one pebble, one grain of sand,
until you know what good and evil
will follow that act.

Ursula K. LeGuin

May 5

The great pleasure in life is
doing what people say you cannot do.

Walter Bagehot

August 28

Kill the snake of doubt in your soul,
crush the worms of fear in your heart
and mountains will move out of your way.

Kate Seredy

May 6

You mustn't force sex to do the work
of love or love to do the work of sex -
that's quite a thought, isn't it?

Mary McCarthy

August 27

Thought for the Day

All that I need to know at any
given moment is revealed to me.
I trust myself and I trust life.
All is well.

May 7

Thought for the Day

When you resent someone,
they live rent-free in your head.

August 26

We never seek things for themselves but for the search.

Blaise Pascal

May 8

We live on the leash of our senses.

Diane Ackerman

August 25

Look everywhere with your eyes;
but with your soul never look at many things,
but at one.

V. V. Rozinov

May 9

Secrets are rarely betrayed or discovered according to any program our fear has sketched out.

George Eliot

August 24

I find the great thing in this world
is not so much where we stand,
as in what direction we are moving.

Goethe

May 10

Thought for the Day

The art of achievement is the
art of making life - YOUR LIFE -
a masterpiece.

August 23

I will open myself up to all the
possibilities around me today,
leaving my fear of change behind.

May 11

When a great poet has lived,
certain things have been done once for all,
and cannot be achieved again.

T.S. Eliot

August 22

A humble knowledge of one's self
is a surer road to God than a
deep searching of the sciences.

Thomas A. Kempis

May 12

When a man comes to me for advice,
I find out the kind of advice he wants,
and I give it to him.

Josh Billings

August 21

You pray in your distress and in your need;
would that you might pray also in the
fullness of your joy and in
your days of abundance.

Kahlil Gibran

May 13

Today, I will favor giving instead of getting.

August 20

Thought for the Day

I celebrate myself today. I am alive.
I am growing. I am willing to do all I am
able to do, to be the best of who I am.

May 14

W hen one's own problems are unsolvable
and all best efforts frustrated,
it is lifesaving to listen to
other people's problems.

Suzanne Massie

August 19

When we are unable to find tranquility within ourselves it is useless to seek it elsewhere.

Duc de La Rochefoucauld

May 15

Nothing contributes so much to tranquilize
the mind as a steady purpose -
a point on which the soul may
fix its intellectual eye.

Mary Shelley

August 18

We are here to add what we can to life,
not to get what we want from it.

William Osler

May 16

Music has been my playmate, my lover, and my crying towel.

Buffy Sainte-Marie

August 17

When one tugs at a single thing in nature, he finds it attached to the rest of the world.

John Muir

May 17

The moment you have in your heart this extraordinary thing called love and feel the depth, the delight, the ecstasy of it, you will discover that for you the world is transformed.

J. Krishnamurti

August 16

The universe is change;
our life is what our thoughts make of it.

Marcus Aurelius

May 18

Those who bring sunshine to the lives
of others cannot keep it from themselves.

James Barrie

August 15

Each friend represents a world in us,
a world possibly not born until they arrive,
and it is only by this meeting that a
new world is born.

Anais Nin

May 19

Thought for the Day

Search for beauty everywhere,
in a flower, a mountain, a machine,
a sonnet and a symphony.

August 14

Today I choose to go with the flow.

May 20

Do you know the hallmark
of the second-rater?
It's resentment of another
man's achievement.

August 13

I always felt that the great high privilege, relief and comfort of friendship was that one had to explain nothing.

Katherine Mansfield

May 21

Love opens the doors into everything, as far as I can see, including and perhaps most of all, the door into one's own secret, an often terrible and frightening, real self.

May Sarton

August 12

Nobody has ever measured, even poets,
how much a heart can hold.

Zelda Fitzgerald

May 22

If there were any justice in the world,
people would be able to fly
over pigeons for a change.

Anonymous

August 11

Thought for the Day

Today my heart brings me to new places
of giving and sharing that I
have not yet experienced.

May 23

Thought for the Day

Each moment of your life is a
brush stroke in the painting
of your growing career.

August 10

I came into this world,
not chiefly to make this a
good place to live in,
but to live in it, be it good or bad.

H. D. Thoreau

May 24

Don't compromise yourself.
You are all you've got.

Betty Ford

August 9

We have our brush and colors - paint Paradise and in we go.

Nikos Kazantzakis

May 25

Once you have learned to love,
you will have learned to live.

August 8

Some people will never learn anything,
for this reason, because they
understand everything too soon.

Alexander Pope

May 26

Thought for the Day

I'll remember: Today I'm a student and
my experiences are my teachers.

August 7

Today I will honor my own values
and be open to change as
a result of growth.

May 27

In the mountains of truth
you never climb in vain.

Nietzsche

August 6

Thought for the Day

Today I will try to focus on any issues that arise. I will put off making important decisions rather than give hasty answers.

May 28

The more sand that has escaped from
the hourglass of our life,
the clearer we should see through it.

Jean Paul

August 5

Imagination has always had the powers
of resurrection that no science can match.

Ingrid Bengis

May 29

Accidents exist only in our heads,
in our limited perceptions.
They are the reflection of the limit
of our knowledge.

Franz Kafka

August 4

To be happy means to be free,
not from pain or fear,
but from care or anxiety.

W.H. Auden

May 30

Life offstage has sometimes been a
wilderness of unpredictables
in an unchoreographed world.

Margot Fonteyn

August 3

Every worthwhile accomplishment,
big or little, has its stages of drudgery
and triumph; a beginning,
a struggle, and a victory.

Anonymous

May 31

Develop a playful attitude
toward problems;
toss them around; handle them
with a light touch.

August 2

Eternity is called whole,
not because it has parts,
but because it is lacking in nothing.

Thomas Aquinas

June 1

Life without love is like a tree
without blossom and fruit.

Kahlil Gibran

August 1

With an open mind, you will be open hearted.
Being open hearted, you will act royally.
Being royal, you will attain the divine.

Tao Te Ching

June 2

Life is like a great jazz riff.
You sense the end the very moment
you were wanting it to go on forever.

Sheila Ballantyne

July 31

Thoughts held in mind produce their kind.

Anonymous

June 3

Good actions are the invisible hinges
on the doors of heaven.

Victor Hugo

July 30

Thought for the Day

The choice is my own.
I'll find happiness and
good will if I foster it.

June 4

I'll take slow, sure steps today and
know I'm on the right path.

July 29

All great reforms require one to dare a lot to win a little.

William L. O'Neill

June 5

Forgive yourself for dreaming larger
than you have lived.

Carol Ann Morrow

July 28

...be patient toward all that is unsolved
in your heart and try to love the questions
themselves like locked rooms and like
books that are written in a
very foreign tongue.

Rainer Maria Rilke

June 6

There are some things you
learn best in calm and some in storm.

Willa Cather

July 27

Thought for the Day

I love me because of all that I am,
not just a part of me. I accept myself
just as I am and that feels so good.

June 7

Thought for the Day

I can be excited about the chance
to celebrate myself today.
My qualities are special
and deserve recognition.

July 26

Happiness is not a matter of events; it depends upon the tides of the mind.

Alice Meynell

June 8

You take people as far as they will go,
not as far as you would like them to go.

Jeannette Rankin

July 25

Believe that life is worth living, and your belief will help create the fact.

William James

June 9

Love is everything. It is the key to life,
and its influences are those
that move the world.

Ralph Waldo Trine

July 24

Mistakes are part of the dues one pays for a full life.

Sophia Loren

June 10

Cherish your visions and your dreams
as they are the children of your soul;
the blueprints of your
ultimate achievements.

Napoleon Hill

July 23

Thought for the Day

I need courage to face the truth;
and the truth will strengthen me.

June 11

When you cease to dream, you cease to live.

Malcolm S. Forbes

July 22

Expand your vision until it includes
the whole earth as your home.

June 12

Thought for the Day

My dreams are my guides
but I must follow them.

July 21

Silence is another form of sound.

Jane Hollister Wheelwright

June 13

Thought for the Day

Nobody's perfect;
such is the nature of my humanity.

July 20

Thought for the Day

My actions today should reflect my
own concerns and be appropriate
to the need.

June 14

Love is the immortal flow of energy
that nourishes, extends and preserves.
Its eternal goal is life.

Smiley Blanton

July 19

Thought for the Day

Your attitude can turn you around today -
for better or for worse.

June 15

Each new season grows from the
leftovers from the past.
That is the essence of change,
and change is the basic law.

Hal Borland

July 18

Our aspirations are our possibilities.

Robert Browning

June 16

It is better to deserve honors and
not have them than to have them
and not deserve them.

Mark Twain

July 17

Getting started can be very hard
for people who have trouble with beginnings.
After all, where do beginnings begin?

Dorothy Bryant

June 17

I believe that it is harder still to be just toward oneself than toward others.

Andre Gide

July 16

My mission on earth is to
recognize the void -
inside and outside of me -
and fill it.

Rabbi Menahem

June 18

When you hold resentment toward another,
you are bound to that person or condition
by an emotional link that is
stronger than steel.

Catherine Ponder

July 15

Thought for the Day

When you take yourself so seriously,
you put on an emotional straitjacket.

June 19

I will set aside my judgment of others
and concentrate instead on freeing myself.

July 14

Begin to see what "is" in front of you,
rather than what you learned is there.

June 20

Life is a battle in which we fall from wounds we receive in running away.

William L. Sullivan

July 13

One word frees us of all the
weight and pain of life: that word is love.

Sophocles (c. 495-406 B.C.)

June 21

A loving person lives in a loving world.
A hostile person lives in a hostile world.
Everyone you meet is your mirror.

Ken Keyes, Jr.

July 12

We can do no great things - only small things with great love.

Mother Teresa

June 22

Today, I'll keep in mind
that achievement is risky,
but dedication
wonderfully liberating.

July 11

Thought for the Day

If you can find a path with no obstacles
it probably doesn't lead anywhere.

June 23

Today's events will remind me who I am.
I will accept them with humor.

July 10

Art is the only way to run away without leaving home.

Twyla Tharp

June 24

Friendship is almost always the union
of a part of one mind with a part of another: People
are friends in spots.

George Santayana

July 9

A sound mind in a sound body is a short but full description of a happy state in this world.

John Locke

June 25

All our resolves and decisions are made in a mood or frame of mind which is certain to change.

Marcel Proust

July 8

Thought for the Day

By unburdening ourselves of our secrets,
we can bring our self image up to date.

June 26

Thought for the Day

I need to concern myself
with today, only. And live it well.

July 7

Thought for the Day

Patience is a tree whose root is bitter,
but its fruit is very sweet.

June 27

Only in growth, reform, and change,
paradoxically enough,
is true security to be found.

Anne Morrow Lindbergh

July 6

To admit I have been wrong is but
saying that I am wiser today
than I was yesterday.

Allan Picket

June 28

There are no grades of vanity,
there are only grades of ability
in concealing it.

Mark Twain

July 5

Look for a long time at what pleases you,
and for a longer time at what pains you.

Colette

June 29

My efforts in my own behalf
are never wasted.

July 4

Let the world know you as you are,
not as you think you should be,
because sooner or later, if you are posing,
you will forget the pose,
and then where are you?

Fanny Brice

June 30

Character is much easier
kept than recovered.

Thomas Paine

July 3

The more abstract the truth
you want to teach,
the more thoroughly you must seduce
the senses to accept it.

Freidrich Nietzsche

July 1

Procrastination is the thief of time.

Edward Young

July 2

Each Day A New Beginning

Friend Forever

Golf Forever ... Work Whenever

Home Is Where The Heart Is

Seasonings

To A Very Special Dad

To A Very Special Mom

Teachers Are "First Class!"

Other Books by Great Quotations

A Light Heart Lives Long

Better Place.

Food For Thought

Golden Years, Golden Words

Heal The World - Make It A

Hollywords

Reflections

Sports Page

Women on Men

Ancient Echoes

Birthday Wishes

Don't Marry, Be Happy

Great Quotes Great Comedians

Harvest Of Thoughts

Love Streams

The Best Of Business Humor

To A Very Special Husband

Who Really Said

Works of Heart